Lerner SPORTS

SUPER SPORTS
TEAMS

T0004823

INSIDE THE
LOS ANGELES
DODGERS

JON M. FISHMAN

Lerner Publications ◆ Minneapolis

SPORTS THRILLS
MEET
RESEARCH SKILLS

Lerner SPORTS

Free Database Trial: **lernersports.com**

Lerner Publications Company
An imprint of Lerner Publishing Group, Inc.
241 First Avenue North
Minneapolis, MN 55401 USA

For reading levels and more information, look up this title at www.lernerbooks.com.

Main body text set in Aptifer Slab LT Pro / Typeface provided by Linotype AG.

Editor: Brianna Kaiser **Designer:** Kimberly Morales **Photo Editor:** Brianna Kaiser

Library of Congress Cataloging-in-Publication Data

Names: Fishman, Jon M., author.
Title: Inside the Los Angeles Dodgers / Jon M. Fishman.
Description: Minneapolis: Lerner Publications, [2022] | Series: Super sports teams (Lerner sports) | Includes bibliographical references and index. | Audience: Ages 7–11 | Audience: Grades 4–6 | Summary: "In this action-packed title, readers will learn all about the Los Angeles Dodgers. Explore the Dodgers' defining moments and discover intriguing facts about how the team, and baseball, have changed over time" —Provided by publisher.
Identifiers: LCCN 2021014655 (print) | LCCN 2021014656 (ebook) | ISBN 9781728441740 (library binding) | ISBN 9781728449463 (paperback) | ISBN 9781728445199 (ebook)
Subjects: LCSH: Los Angeles Dodgers (Baseball team)—Juvenile literature.
Classification: LCC GV875.L6 F57 2022 (print) | LCC GV875.L6 (ebook) | DDC 796.357/640979494—dc23

LC record available at https://lccn.loc.gov/2021014655
LC ebook record available at https://lccn.loc.gov/2021014656

Manufactured in the United States of America
1-49929-49772-8/12/2021

TABLE OF CONTENTS

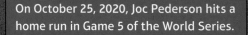

On October 25, 2020, Joc Pederson hits a home run in Game 5 of the World Series.

SEVEN-TIME CHAMPIONS

FACTS AT A GLANCE

- The Dodgers joined the **NATIONAL LEAGUE (NL)** in 1890.

- **THE DODGERS** took their nickname from trolley dodgers in Brooklyn, New York.

- The team has won seven **WORLD SERIES**.

- **DODGER STADIUM** is the third-oldest Major League Baseball (MLB) stadium.

For years, the Los Angeles Dodgers were one of the best teams in MLB. They played in the World Series in 2017 and 2018, but they lost both times. In 2020, the Dodgers had the chance to turn their luck around.

Dodgers outfielder Joc Pederson stepped forward and took a massive swing in Game 5 of the 2020 World Series. *Crack!* With the bat still in his hand, he walked slowly toward first base. When the ball flew over the outfield wall for a home run, Pederson dropped the bat and began jogging. His blast helped the Dodgers win the game against the Tampa Bay Rays.

In Game 6, superstar outfielder Mookie Betts stepped up. Betts had played six seasons with the Boston Red Sox and helped them win the 2018 World Series. Before the start of the 2020 season, the Dodgers added

Betts to their roster. Dodgers fans hoped Betts would improve their team's chances of winning the series for the first time in over 30 years.

The Dodgers had a 3–2 series lead over the Rays. Los Angeles needed one more victory to become MLB champions. In the sixth inning, the Rays were ahead 1–0. Betts smacked a double for the Dodgers with teammate Austin Barnes on base. Betts and Barnes later scored to put Los Angeles ahead 2–1.

Betts wasn't finished. In the eighth inning, he blasted a long home run to left-center field. The Dodgers won the game 3–1 and became World Series champions for the seventh time!

Betts's home run helped the Dodgers win Game 6.

Dodgers players celebrate winning the World Series in 2020.

Jackie Robinson poses in his Dodgers uniform. Many fans consider Robinson to be the most important player in Dodgers history.

BECOMING THE DODGERS

In the early 1880s, the Brooklyn Atlantics began playing in Brooklyn, New York. The Atlantics played in the American Association (AA), a pro baseball league. In 1884, they finished in ninth place out of 13 teams.

Six years later, the team moved to the NL. The NL was the top pro league in the US. Brooklyn won their first NL title that year. In 1903, the NL joined the American League (AL) to form MLB.

Brooklyn tried many team names. After the Atlantics, they were the Grays, the Grooms, and the Bridegrooms. For several seasons, the team's nickname was the Superbas. Then they tried the Robins. They finally settled on the Dodgers in 1932.

The Brooklyn Bridegrooms in 1889

In 1941, the Dodgers played in their first World Series. They faced the New York Yankees. After five close games, the Yankees came out on top.

Beginning in the late 1800s, MLB was segregated. The league's white team owners refused to hire Black players or coaches. Black people played and coached in the Negro Leagues. They earned less money and received less attention than MLB players did.

In 1945, Negro Leagues star Jackie Robinson signed a contract with the Dodgers. It was a big step toward ending segregation in MLB.

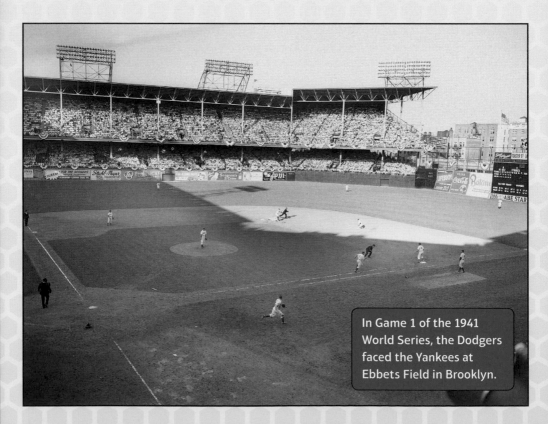

In Game 1 of the 1941 World Series, the Dodgers faced the Yankees at Ebbets Field in Brooklyn.

On April 18, 1946, Robinson (*right*) is greeted by Montreal teammate George Shuba at home plate after Robinson hit a home run.

The next year, Robinson played for the Montreal Royals. The Royals were the top minor-league team of the Dodgers.

On April 15, 1947, Robinson played for the Dodgers in his first MLB game. For the season he had a .297 batting average, stole 29 bases, and won the Rookie of the Year award. MLB segregation slowly ended as more Black players began to join the league.

Robinson helped the Dodgers reach the 1947 World Series. Once again, they fell to the Yankees. Brooklyn played in the World Series in 1949, 1952, and 1953. Each time, the Yankees beat them.

In 1955, Robinson and the Dodgers finally broke through. They topped the Yankees in seven hard-fought World Series games. The two teams faced off again the next year. This time, the Yankees won the series.

Brooklyn had played at Ebbets Field since 1913. The stadium needed repairs. Officials in Los Angeles, California, offered to build a new stadium for the Dodgers if they moved there.

On September 24, 1957, the Dodgers played their last game at Ebbets Field. They moved to California and played at Los Angeles

Robinson slides home to score a run in the 1955 World Series opening game.

Dodger Stadium on April 10, 1962, the day the Los Angeles Dodgers played their first game at their new stadium

Memorial Coliseum until 1961. The following year, they moved into brand-new Dodger Stadium.

In Los Angeles, the Dodgers have enjoyed amazing success. Since leaving New York, they've won six World Series titles. And they've become one of the most famous and valuable teams in the world.

Justin Turner smacks a hit to score a run for the Dodgers in Game 2 of the 2017 National League Championship Series (NLCS).

AMAZING
MOMENTS

In 1959, the Dodgers won their first World Series in Los Angeles. They beat the Chicago White Sox 4–2. Four years later, the Dodgers and the Yankees faced off in the series for the eighth time.

The 1963 Dodgers had the second-best record in MLB—right behind the Yankees. New York rolled through the AL. But they were no match for the NL-champion Dodgers.

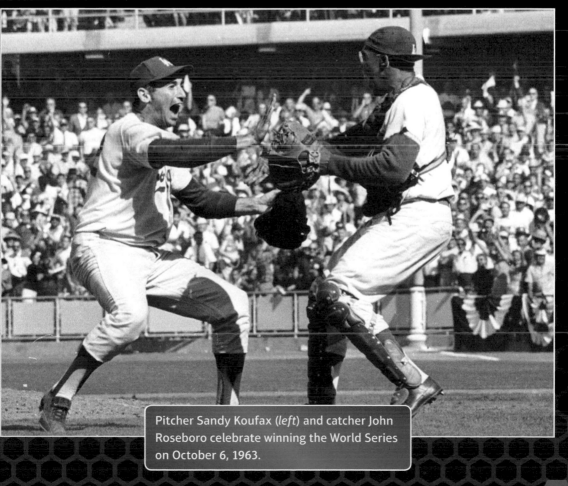

Pitcher Sandy Koufax (*left*) and catcher John Roseboro celebrate winning the World Series on October 6, 1963.

Los Angeles won the first three games. In Game 4, Sandy Koufax threw for the Dodgers. He had been the NL's best pitcher that year. Koufax pitched all nine innings and allowed only one run. The Dodgers won 2–1!

On September 9, 1965, Koufax pitched an even better game. Facing the Chicago Cubs at Dodger Stadium, he didn't allow any opposing hitters to reach base. The 1–0 Dodgers victory was just the sixth perfect game in MLB history.

In 1988, the Dodgers took part in one of the most thrilling plays in World Series history. Kirk Gibson was that year's NL Most Valuable Player (MVP). He helped the Dodgers win the NLCS. But in Game 7 of the NLCS, Gibson hurt his knee sliding into second base.

Koufax pitching his perfect game on September 9, 1965

Gibson sat on the bench for Game 1 of the World Series. He watched the Dodgers fall behind the Oakland Athletics 4–3. With two outs in the ninth inning, the Dodgers were desperate. Manager Tommy Lasorda called on Gibson.

The crowd at Dodger Stadium cheered as Gibson limped to home plate.

The fans loved their MVP, but clearly, he couldn't run fast. Luckily, he didn't need to. Gibson smashed the ball deep to right field. The cheers grew as the ball cleared the fence for a two-run blast. Los Angeles won the game and later the World Series.

After 1988, the Dodgers played 27 seasons without reaching the World Series. In 2017, they battled the Cubs in the NLCS. Game 2 was tied 1–1 in the ninth inning. The Dodgers

Gibson runs the bases after hitting his two-run home run to help the Dodgers win Game 1.

needed another game-winning homer. This time, Justin Turner stepped up. He hit a three-run blast for the win. The Dodgers made it to the World Series but lost to the Houston Astros.

The Boston Red Sox beat Los Angeles in the 2018 World Series. After losing in the first round of the playoffs the next year, the Dodgers reached the 2020 NLCS against the Atlanta Braves. In Game 7, the score was tied 3–3 in the seventh inning.

Dodgers outfielder and first baseman Cody Bellinger batted. He took a huge swing. Bellinger swung so hard that the bat came all the way around to touch his back. *Bang!* As soon as he made contact with the ball, he knew it was gone. Bellinger's blast helped the Dodgers win 4–3 and reach the World Series.

Clayton Kershaw pitches for the Dodgers in the 2020 World Series.

DODGERS SUPERSTARS

Dodgers history is full of incredible players. Fans will never forget stars like Pee Wee Reese, Roy Campanella, Duke Snider, and Don Sutton. But no one made a bigger impact on the team and the sport than Robinson did.

Robinson played for the Dodgers from 1947 to 1956. He won the 1949 NL MVP award, played in six All-Star Games, and helped Brooklyn win the 1955 World Series. For his amazing play on the field, Robinson joined the Baseball Hall of Fame in 1962.

Robinson played for the Dodgers for 10 seasons.

Koufax's MLB career began in 1955. In the early 1960s, he dominated the sport. Koufax won 129 games from 1961 to 1966. He also won two World Series MVP awards and the 1963 NL MVP.

In 1963, Koufax won 25 games and lost only five.

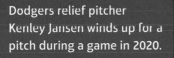

Many fans consider Koufax to be the best pitcher in Dodgers history. One of the few who can challenge him is Clayton Kershaw. He started his MLB career in 2008. By 2014, Kershaw had won three Cy Young Awards as the NL's top pitcher. He cemented his status as an all-time Dodgers great by winning two games in the 2020 World Series.

Kershaw is surrounded by talented teammates. When he leaves a game, big right-handed pitcher Kenley Jansen often takes over. Jansen holds the Dodgers career saves record with more than 300.

Bellinger hits a two-run home run in the first game of the 2020 World Series.

Bellinger is another big reason for the team's recent success. In 2019, he batted .305 with 47 home runs. He won the NL MVP award. Then Bellinger hit four homers in the 2020 playoffs to help the Dodgers reach the World Series.

Dodgers players get ready to run onto the field to celebrate winning the 2020 World Series.

A statue of Jackie Robinson at Dodger Stadium

FAN FAVORITES

Since Dodger Stadium opened in 1962, it has hosted nine World Series and almost 5,000 MLB games. Dodger Stadium is the third-oldest MLB ballpark. It's the oldest baseball stadium west of the Mississippi River.

Dodger Stadium has room for 56,000 fans. Each season, millions of Dodgers fans go to watch their favorite team play at the stadium. In 1978, Dodger Stadium became the first MLB ballpark to have more than three million fans visit in a season.

In 2020, the team spent $100 million to fix up Dodger Stadium. They built Centerfield Plaza. The open area beyond center field is a space for fans to gather, eat, and play. They also added bridges and elevators for fans and put in a new sound system.

Dodger Stadium in Los Angeles

Fans can also admire two legends in Centerfield Plaza. In 2017, the Dodgers built a statue to honor Jackie Robinson. The team moved it to Centerfield Plaza to stand near a new statue of Sandy Koufax.

The Dodgers want their fans to have a great time at the ballpark. Part of the fun is cheering for a winning team. With superstars like Betts and Bellinger leading the way, Dodgers fans have a lot to look forward to.

Bellinger signs baseballs for fans.

Dodgers fans cheer during a game in 2018.

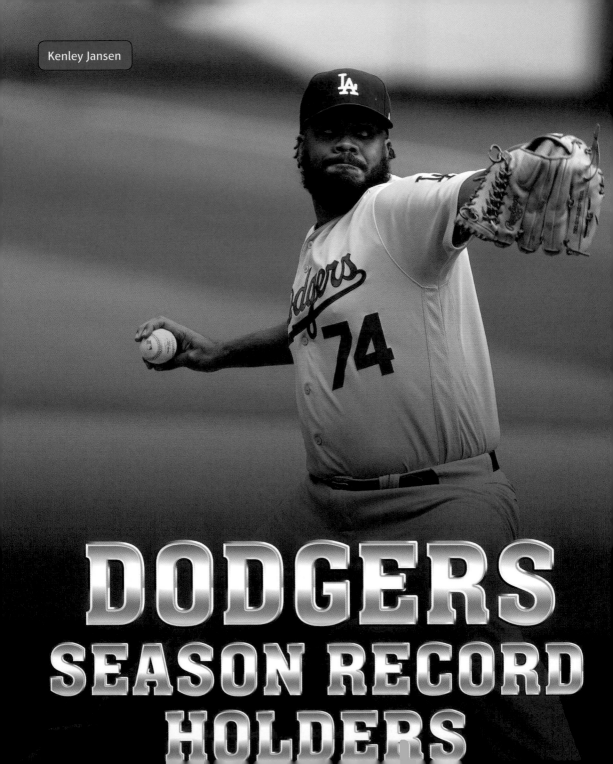

Kenley Jansen

DODGERS
SEASON RECORD
HOLDERS

HITS

1. Babe Herman, 241 (1930)
2. Tommy Davis, 230 (1962)
3. Zack Wheat, 221 (1925)
4. Lefty O'Doul, 219 (1932)
5. Babe Herman, 217 (1929)

HOME RUNS

1. Shawn Green, 49 (2001)
2. Adrian Beltre, 48 (2004)
3. Cody Bellinger, 47 (2019)
4. Gary Sheffield, 43 (2000)
   Duke Snider, 43 (1956)

STOLEN BASES

1. Maury Wills, 104 (1962)
2. Maury Wills, 94 (1965)
3. Darby O'Brien, 91 (1889)
4. John Ward, 88 (1892)
5. Hub Collins, 85 (1890)

WINS

1. Bob Caruthers, 40 (1889)
2. Henry Porter, 33 (1885)
3. Tom Lovett, 30 (1890)
4. Bob Caruthers, 29 (1888)
   George Haddock, 29 (1892)

STRIKEOUTS

1. Sandy Koufax, 382 (1965)
2. Sandy Koufax, 317 (1966)
3. Sandy Koufax, 306 (1963)
4. Clayton Kershaw, 301 (2015)
5. Sandy Koufax, 269 (1961)

SAVES

1. Éric Gagné, 55 (2003)
2. Éric Gagné, 52 (2002)
3. Kenley Jansen, 47 (2016)
4. Éric Gagné, 45 (2004)
5. Kenley Jansen, 44 (2014)
   Todd Worrell, 44 (1996)

GLOSSARY

blast: a home run

contract: a legal agreement

double: a hit that allows the batter to reach second base

minor league: a pro baseball league that is not a major league

Negro Leagues: former baseball leagues that were made up of Black people and other people of color

rookie: a first-year player

roster: a list of the players on a team

save: when a relief pitcher protects a team's lead

segregated: organized to keep members of different races apart, either by dividing facilities into different sections or creating separate facilities for members of certain races

trolley: a streetcar powered by electricity that is used for public transportation

LEARN MORE

Baseball Hall of Fame
https://baseballhall.org/

Dodgers History
https://www.mlb.com/dodgers/history

Leed, Percy. *Sandy Koufax: Lefty Legend*. Minneapolis: Lerner Publications, 2021.

Los Angeles Dodgers
https://www.mlb.com/dodgers

Monson, James. *Behind the Scenes Baseball*. Minneapolis: Lerner Publications, 2020.

Rhodes, Sam. *Los Angeles Dodgers*. New York: AV2 by Weigl, 2018.

INDEX

PHOTO ACKNOWLEDGMENTS

Image credits: AP Photo/David J. Phillip, p. 4; AP Photo/Kydpl Kyodo, pp. 6, 18, 22; AP Photo/Tony Gutierrez, pp. 7, 23; Science History Images/Alamy Stock Photo, p. 8; Niday Picture Library/Alamy Stock Photo, p. 9; AP Photo/ Uncredited, p. 10; AP Photo/John Lent, p. 11; AP Photo/John Rooney, p. 12; AP Photo, pp. 13, 15; AP Photo/Mark J. Terrill, p. 14; AP Photo/HPM, p. 16; AP Photo/Rusty Kennedy, p. 17; Science History Images/Alamy Stock Photo, p. 19; AP Photo/David Durochik, p. 20; AP Photo/Ted S. Warren, p. 21; Vitaly Loz/Shutterstock.com, p. 24; Emma_Griffiths/Shutterstock.com, p. 25; UPI/ Alamy Stock Photo, p. 26; Joseph Sohm/Shutterstock.com, p. 27; AP Photo/ Jeff Chiu, p. 28.

Design element: Master3D/Shutterstock.com.

Cover: Alex Trautwig/MLB Photos/Getty Images.